Someone I Know Lives in Prison

by Rebecca Myers

illustrated by John G. Crews

Copyright © 2013 Rebecca Myers

Ordering contact: MyersRL2@me.com

Incarceration goes far beyond the offender; it enormously affects the children and family of the offender. I thank Lisa Jones, Constituent Services Officer at the Missouri Department of Corrections for helping me to know I was on the right path to publish this book.

I dedicate this book to my father whose size 13 feet were never too big to walk in the shoes of someone else.
- R.M.

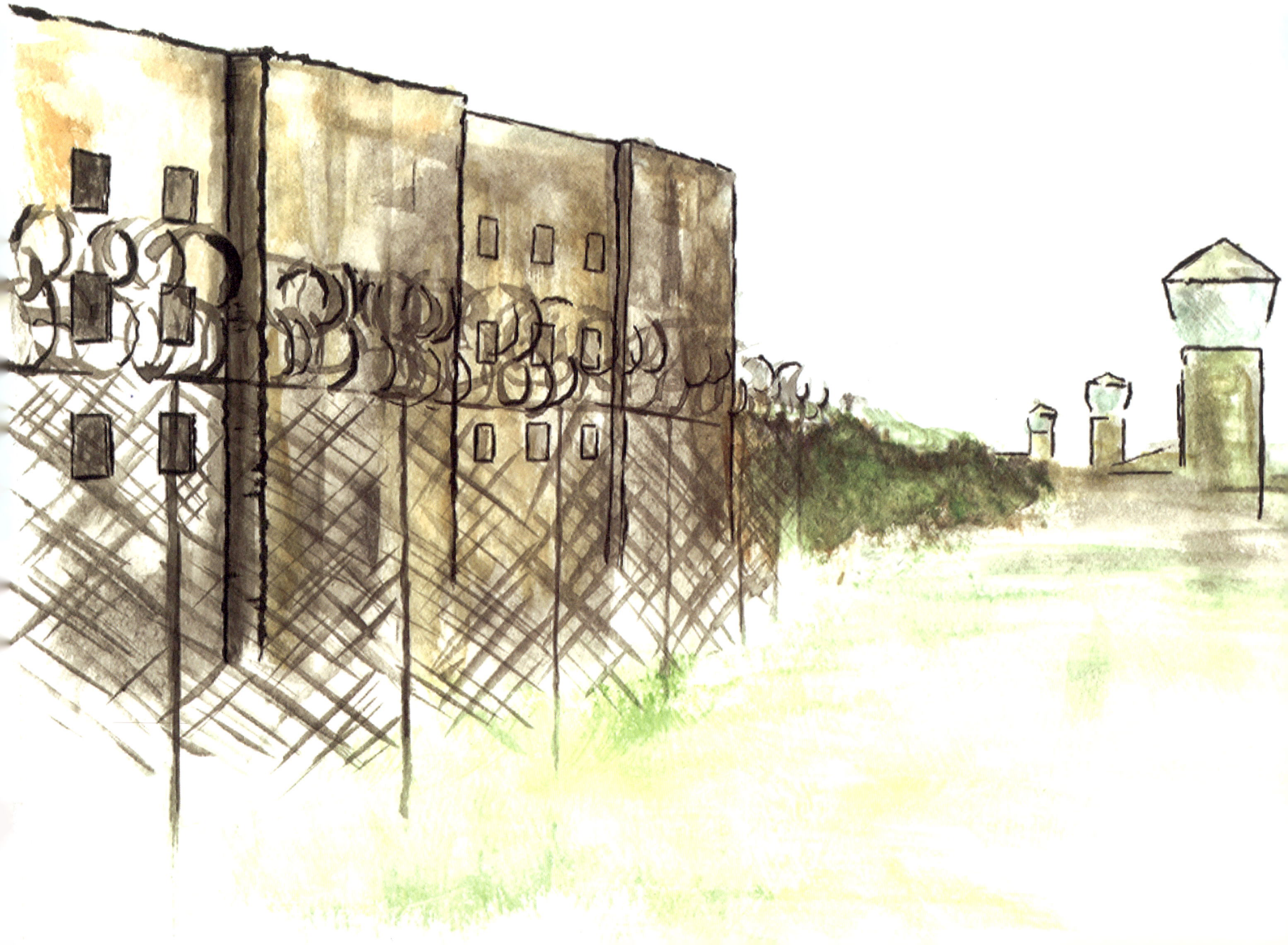

Someone in my family lives in a place called prison.
Prison is a big building with a tall fence around it so only
certain people can come in or leave.

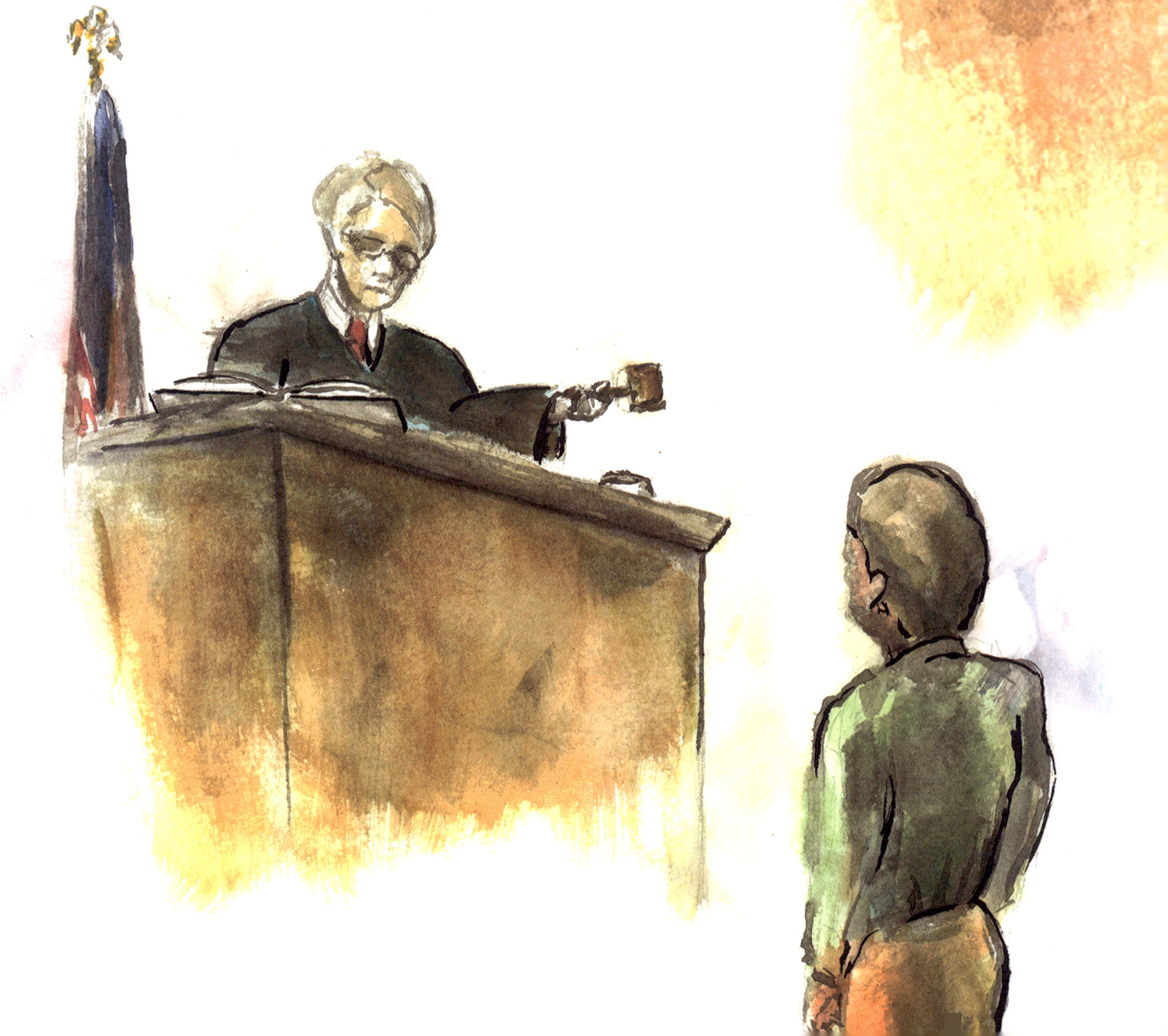

People who live in prison have been found guilty of making a bad choice. They have been told to live in prison for a short time or a long time. They must leave their home and family behind and live in prison, where bad choices cannot easily be made again.

Prisons have special visiting days for family and friends. When you visit a person in prison, you must follow the prison rules. One rule is that you wear clothes that cover most of your skin.

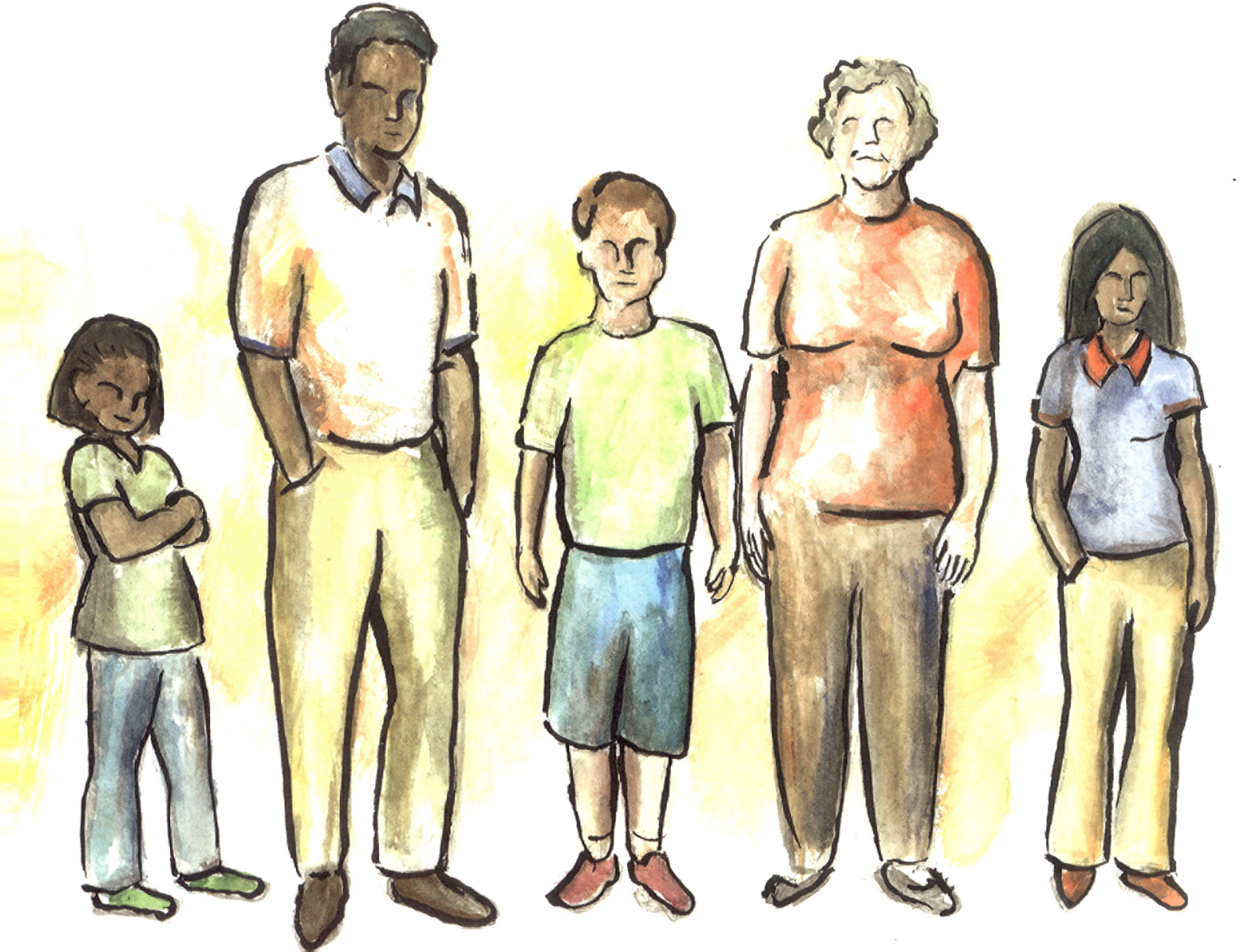

The men and women who take turns watching the people in prison are called corrections officers. They wear uniforms.

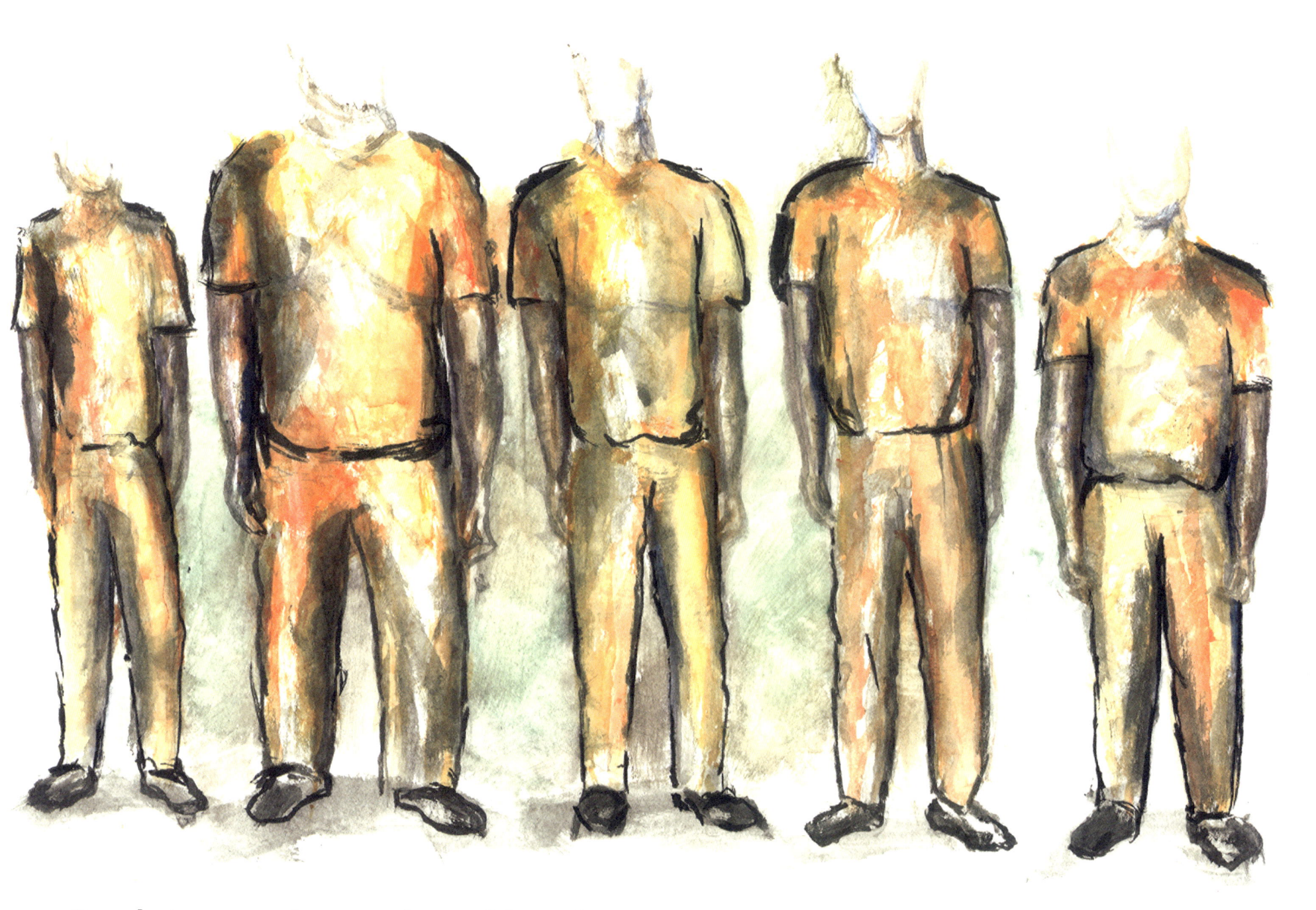

People in prison have to dress alike. They even wear the same kind of shoes and coats.

It seems to take a long time in the car when we drive to prison from our house. When we get there, we park in the parking lot and follow the prison visiting rules.

Visitors must leave all of their things in
the car. They do not get to take a purse, phone,
food, books, games, sunglasses, or other things
into the visiting room. Some prisons let visitors
bring a see-through bag with money in it so they
can buy food and a drink while visiting. It is simple when you visit prison because only
people matter, not the things that were left in the car.

Visitors write their name on a paper. This lets the corrections officer know who you are and who you want to visit.

You may have to wait in line as people take turns to stand in front of a corrections officer, who will make sure everyone is following the prison rules. If a scanner machine is used, visitors will take a small cloth and wipe it across their clothes to make sure their clothes are clean.

A corrections officer may have each visitor walk through a doorway that is a metal detector.

There is also another metal detector that looks like a wand and it may be pointed at each person. If a metal detector makes a beeping noise, it means a person forgot to take something out of his or her pocket or shoes.

The corrections officer may place a stamp on each visitor's hand before they go through the locked doors to the visiting room.

The visiting room is filled with tables and chairs so families can sit together.

During our visit, we take the time to look at each other and listen to each other as we talk about everything we did while we missed each other.

We must use our softer voices as we talk at our table. Sometimes we draw pictures and color together.

During visiting hours, we use the money from the see-through bag to buy things to eat and drink. There are several vending machines and we buy sandwiches, chips, candy, and a drink so we can eat together as a family.

Corrections officers are in the visiting room and they walk around and watch everybody visit.

When it is time to leave, it is hard to say good-bye. Most people hug, some people cry, and all people wish things were different.

We leave with our empty see-through bags, go through the locked prison doors, show our stamped hands, take back our car keys, and walk outside to the parking lot and drive home.

Someone in my family lives in prison, and because of that my life has changed.